Living in space

Katie Daynes
Designed by Zoe Wray

Illustrated by Christyan Fox and Alex Pang

Space consultant: Stuart Atkinson

Reading consultant: Alison Kelly,
Roehampton University

Contents

3   Earth and space
4   Space school
6   Preparing to go
8   Lift off
10   In orbit
12   A home in space
14   The space station
16   Eating and drinking
18   Keeping clean
20   A day in space
22   Spacesuits
24   Going outside
26   Back to Earth
28   Space trips
30   Glossary of space words
31   Web sites to visit
32   Index

Earth and space

The Earth is a big round planet.
This is what it looks like from space.

Astronauts travel into space to live and work.

The word astronaut means
"star sailor".

Space school

To become an astronaut, you have to go to space school and learn how to live in space.

On Earth when things jump they go up and then down.

An invisible force called gravity pulls them down.

In space there is very little gravity so everything floats.

Astronauts need lots of training to know what to do when they float in space.

At space school, astronauts learn how to work while floating in water. It feels like working in space.

Astronauts also try out emergency escapes.

They slide down a pole onto a soft mat.

Preparing to go

Astronauts fly to space in a space shuttle. The shuttle leaves from a launch pad.

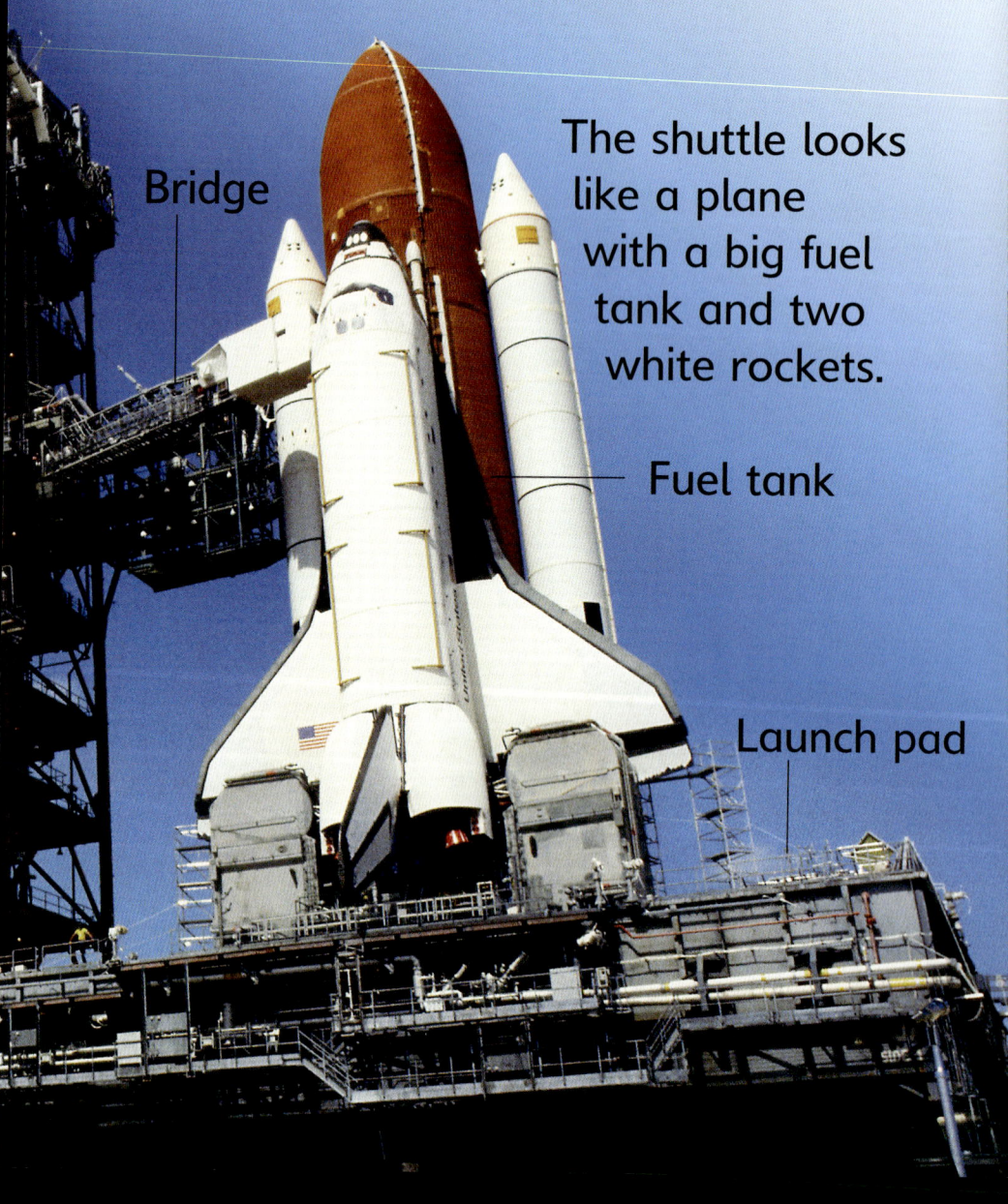

Bridge

The shuttle looks like a plane with a big fuel tank and two white rockets.

Fuel tank

Launch pad

The astronauts put on special orange suits.

They travel to the shuttle in an elevator.

Then they cross a bridge into the shuttle.

The astronauts lie in the nose of the shuttle and wait until it's time to go.

Lift off

The engines start burning fuel from the fuel tank. Then the two rockets light up and the shuttle zooms into space.

3... 2... 1... Lift off!

Nobody is allowed to stand close to the launch pad because it is too dangerous.

After two minutes, the rockets fall into the sea.

After eight minutes, the fuel tank falls away.

The shuttle is now floating in space.

Two flaps open up on the back of the shuttle so it doesn't get too hot inside.

In orbit

The space shuttle goes around the Earth in a big circle. This is known as being in orbit.

It only takes 90 minutes for the shuttle to orbit the Earth.

The middle part of the shuttle is called the payload bay. It carries big objects into space.

The astronauts work, eat and sleep in the nose of the shuttle.

A home in space

Some astronauts stay in space for a long time. They live in a floating home called a space station.

Astronauts are building a big, new space station. This is what it will look like when it's finished.

The shuttle travels through space.

It flies close to the space station.

Then it joins onto the space station.

When the space station is finished, it will be as big as two soccer fields.

The space station

The space shuttle carries the parts for the new space station into space.

A robot arm on the shuttle picks a big tube out of the payload bay.

The robot arm then joins the new tube onto the space station.

Some of the tubes are as big as a bus.

The astronauts live in a tube like this.

Bedroom

Toilet

Shower

Eating area

They wear everyday clothes in the space station.

Eating and drinking

When astronauts go into space they take their food and drinks with them.

The first meals taken to space didn't look or taste very nice.

Beef with vegetables

Food was dried and sealed up.

Astronauts added warm water...

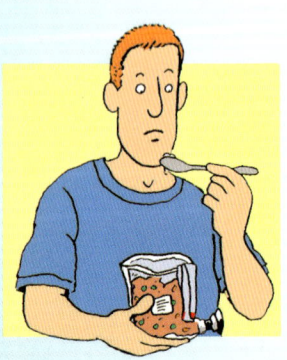

...which made the food soggy.

Can you see the blob of drink floating to the astronaut's mouth?

Today, most space meals come already prepared in trays. They just need to be heated. Fruit is dried to keep it fresh.

Dried strawberries

The first man to walk on the Moon ate dried ice cream in space.

Keeping clean

It is difficult living in a space station. There is not much room and everything floats.

In a space shower the water flows out then floats in blobs.

An astronaut holds onto the handle to keep still while he washes.

After rinsing, he uses a hose to suck up all the water.

A space toilet has bars and foot rests to help the astronaut sit down.

An astronaut slides the bars over her legs and turns on the air flow.

Astronauts recycle some water in space and more comes from Earth in tanks like these.

A day in space

Astronauts work in the space station. Some work in a laboratory, like the one below. It's a tube where they can carry out tests.

They also fit new parts inside the space station.

They exercise every day to keep fit and healthy.

They sleep in a sleeping bag attached to the wall.

When they're not working, astronauts read, listen to music, or just look at the amazing views of Earth.

Astronauts can talk to people on Earth and send messages by computer.

Spacesuits

When astronauts work outside the space station they have to wear a spacesuit.

The first layer keeps them cool or warm.

They add an outer layer for protection.

The helmet and gloves go on last.

Inside their helmets astronauts can drink through a straw and talk to each other.

Straw

A backpack carries air to breathe and water to warm or cool the astronaut.

Space boots aren't made for walking. The astronauts move around by holding onto things with their hands.

Going outside

Astronauts go out into space through an airlock. It stops air from escaping from the space station.

An astronaut goes through the first door.

In the airlock he puts on a spacesuit.

He leaves through the second door.

An astronaut sometimes puts on a jet pack so he can move around outside the space station.

When astronauts work outside it is called spacewalking. This astronaut is spacewalking in the shuttle's payload bay.

One astronaut dropped a glove in space. It is still floating around somewhere.

Back to Earth

After 90 days on the space station the astronauts travel back to Earth.

The shuttle leaves the space station.

It heats up as it drops back through the air.

The shuttle lands on a runway like a plane.

A parachute helps it to slow down.

The longest an astronaut has stayed in space is one year and 72 days.

Space trips

The first trip to space was in 1957.

The first living thing to travel from Earth to space was a dog named Laika.

In 1969 astronauts walked on the moon for the first time.

There is no wind or rain on the Moon, so footprints stay for hundreds of years.

In the future you may be able to fly into space in a space plane like this.

People might also live in space homes like this.

Exercise area

Bedroom

Eating area

Glossary of space words

Here are some of the words in this book you might not know. This page tells you what they mean.

 planet - a huge round object in space. The Earth is a planet.

 gravity - an invisible force that pulls things on Earth down to the ground.

 fuel - something which burns to give the shuttle power to move very fast.

 in orbit - going around a planet in a big circle.

 payload bay - the middle part of the shuttle where big objects are carried.

 laboratory - a place where people carry out tests.

 airlock - a set of doors for getting into and out of a space station or shuttle.

Websites to visit

You can visits exciting websites to find out more about living in space.

To visit these websites, go to the Usborne Quicklinks Website at **www.usborne-quicklinks.com** Read the internet safety guidelines, and then type the keywords "**beginners space**".

The websites are regularly reviewed and the links in Usborne Quicklinks are updated. However, Usborne Publishing in not responsible, and does not accept liability, for the content or availability of any website other than its own. We recommend that children are supervised while on the internet.

The shiny visor on this helmet reflects sunlight to protect the astronaut's eyes.

Index

airlock, 24, 30
bedroom, 15, 29
drink, 16-17, 22
Earth, 3, 4, 11, 12, 19, 21, 26, 28, 30
eating, 11, 15, 16-17, 29
exercise, 21, 29
food, 16-17
fuel tank, 6, 8, 9
gravity, 4, 30
jet pack, 24
laboratory, 20, 30
Moon, 17, 28
orbit, 10, 11, 30
parachute, 27
payload bay, 11, 25, 30
rockets, 6, 8, 9
shower, 15, 18
shuttle, 6, 7, 8, 9, 10, 11, 13, 14, 25, 26, 30
space station, 12-13, 14-15, 18, 20, 22, 24, 26, 30
spacesuits, 22-23, 24
spacewalking, 25
toilet, 15, 19
water, 5, 16, 18, 19, 23

Acknowledgements

Cover design: Nicola Butler

Photo credits

The publishers are grateful to the following for permission to reproduce material:
© **Bristol Spaceplanes** 29, © **Corbis** (Richard T. Nowitz) 4, (Bettmann) 6, (Digital image © 1996 CORBIS; Original image courtesy of NASA/CORBIS) 9, (Bettmann) 16, (Roger Ressmeyer) 19, © **Digital Vision** Cover, 3, 26, © **Genesis Space Photo Library** 7, 19, © **NASA** Cover, 1, 5, 8, 12-13, 19, 20, 21, 23, 24, 25, 26-27, 28, 31

With thanks to

Katie Towers at Buxton Foods Ltd for the space strawberries.

Every effort has been made to trace and acknowledge ownership of copyright. If any rights have been omitted, the publishers offer to rectify this in any subsequent editions following notification.

First published in 2002 by Usborne Publishing Ltd., Usborne House, 83-85 Saffron Hill, London EC1N 8RT, England. www.usborne.com Copyright © 2006, 2002 Usborne Publishing Ltd. The name Usborne and the devices are Trade Marks of Usborne Publishing Ltd. All rights reserved. No part of this publication may be reproduced, stored in a retrieval system, or transmitted in any form or by any means, electronic, mechanical, photocopying, recording or otherwise without the prior permission of the publisher.
First published in America 2003. U.E. Printed in China.